NATURAL WORLD

GIRAFFE

HABITATS • LIFE CYCLES • FOOD CHAINS • THREATS

Michael Leach

RAINTREE
STECK-VAUGHN
RSVP® PUBLISHERS

A Harcourt Company

Austin   New York
www.raintreesteckvaughn.com

NATURAL WORLD

Chimpanzee • Crocodile • Black Rhino • Dolphin • Elephant
Giant Panda • Giraffe • Golden Eagle • Great White Shark
Grizzly Bear • Hippopotamus • Killer Whale • Leopard • Lion
Orangutan • Penguin • Polar Bear • Tiger

Cover: A male giraffe, up close.
Title page: A giraffe wanders across its territory in front of Mount Kilimanjaro, Africa's highest mountain, in northern Tanzania.
Contents page: Giraffes are very easy to approach in the wild. They often show an interest in visitors.
Index page: A young giraffe eating leaves from the top of a bush.

Published by Raintree Steck-Vaughn Publishers,
an imprint of Steck-Vaughn Company

Library of Congress Cataloging-in-Publication Data
Leach, Michael.
Giraffe : habitats, life cycles, food chains, threats / Michael Leach.
    p.   cm.-- (Natural world)
    Includes bibliographical references (p.).
    ISBN 0-7398-4435-0
    1. Giraffe--Juvenile literature. [1. Giraffe] I. Title. II. Natural world (Austin, Tex.)

    QL737.U56 L43 2001
    599.638--dc21   2001018573

Printed in Italy. Bound in the United States
1 2 3 4 5 6 7 8 9 0 LB 05 04 03 02 01

Picture acknowledgments
Ardea 9 Ferrero-Labat, 15 Ian Beames, 23, 28, 34 Ferrero-Labat, 45 (top) Ian Beames, 45 (bottom) Ferrero-Labat, 48 Ferrero-Labat; *Bruce Coleman* Contents page Christer Fredriksson, 18 Renee Lynn, 20 Gunter Kohler, 25 Luiz Claudio Marigo, 32 HPH Photography; *Corbis* 19 Tom Nebbia, 33 Mary Ann McDonald, 37 Karl Amman, 38 Peter Johnson, 41 Anthony Bannister/Gallo Image; *Digital Vision* 27, 35; *Getty Images* 12, 44 (middle) J Sneesby/B Wilkins, 22 Howie Garber, 30 Art Wolfe, 31 Renee Lynn; *NHPA* Front cover Martin Harvey, 6 Steve Robinson, 7 Gerard Lacz, 13 Stephen Krasemann, 14 John Shaw, 16, 17 Nigel J Dennis, 21 Anthony Bannister, 24 Nigel J Dennis, 29 Daryl Balfour, 36 Nigel J Dennis, 39 Martin Harvey, 40 Christophe Ratier, 42 G I Bernard, 43 Joe Blossom, 44 (bottom) John Shaw, 45 (middle) Nigel J Dennis; *Oxford Scientific Films* 8; *Still Pictures* 10, 11, 44 (top) Nicholas Granier. Artwork by Michael Posen.

Contents

Meet the Giraffe

Giraffes are the tallest animals on earth. They were once found over most of Africa, but now live only south of the Sahara Desert. They are sociable animals that live together in loose herds, in open woodlands.

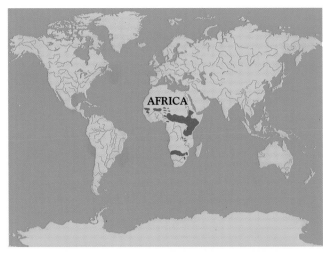

AFRICA

▲ The red shading on this map shows where giraffes live in Africa.

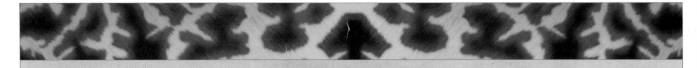

GIRAFFE FACTS

Male giraffes are known as bulls and can grow up to 18 feet (5.3 m) tall at head height. Females are known as cows and grow up to 15 feet (4.5 m) tall.

●

Males weigh up to 4,255 pounds (1,930 kg), while females weigh up to 2,600 pounds (1,180 kg).

●

The Latin name for the giraffe is *Giraffa camelopardalis*. The word *"camelopardalis"* comes from an old name for giraffes: camel-leopards, because they are shaped like camels and have the spots of leopards. The word *giraffe* comes from the Arabic word *zirafah*, which means *fast walker*.

Horns

The giraffe's horns are covered in skin, with a tuft of thick black hair on top. Some giraffes have only two horns, but others have four: two large and two small. There is sometimes an extra horn in the centre. The horns continue to grow throughout the giraffe's life.

Eyes and ears

Giraffes have excellent eyesight and hearing.

Nostrils

Giraffes have a good sense of smell. They can close their narrow nostrils to keep out sand and dust in dust-storms, or to keep out flies.

Neck

The neck can be over 6 feet (1.8 m) long. A short mane grows along the neck.

Lips and tongue

A giraffe's sensitive lips act like fingers, delicately pulling off leaves and putting them into its mouth. The lips are rough to help grip smooth leaves. Giraffes have a long tongue of up to 18 inches (45 cm), which can be wound around leaves and pulled down for eating. Like the lips, the end of the tongue is rough to help grip smooth leaves.

Legs

A giraffe's legs can be over 6 feet (1.8 m) long. They help it run up to 37 miles (60 km) an hour and are strong for powerful defensive kicks.

Tail

Giraffe's tails are about 3 feet (1 m) long with a tuft of long black hairs at the end. They are flicked around to drive away flies.

Hooves

A giraffe's hooves are split into two parts.

▶ An adult giraffe

Habitat

Giraffes live in dry grasslands that contain a large number of trees or woodlands. They never wander far into forests or true desert, but are found in very arid areas. The broken, light-brown pattern of a giraffe's coat is excellent camouflage. When standing completely still amongst the dappled shadows of a tree, a giraffe can be surprisingly difficult to spot.

PATTERN

No two giraffes are identical. Each has its own unique set of stripes and spots. The pattern is as distinctive as a fingerprint and stays with the giraffe throughout its life. This makes it easy for scientists to follow and study individual giraffes. The markings of all giraffes grow darker as they get older.

Relatives

Giraffes are members of the family known as *giraffiadae*, which contains only one other species: the okapi. The okapi is a shy animal that lives in the rain forests of the Congo basin in Central Africa. It looks a bit like a giraffe with a much shorter neck. Very little is known about the behavior of wild okapis. The rain forest is so thick that they are extremely difficult to study.

Okapis are hunted by the pygmy tribes that live in Central Africa, so they have learned to fear humans. Like their taller cousins, okapi have very sensitive eyes, ears and noses. They are quick to detect the presence of people and usually disappear into the forest long before they are seen.

▲ The okapi is much smaller than a giraffe. It measures just 5.6 feet (1.7 m) high and weighs 551 pounds (250 kg).

◄ Giraffes are covered with very short hair. This keeps off small biting insects and protects the skin against the hot African sun.

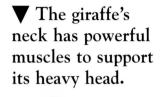

▼ The giraffe's neck has powerful muscles to support its heavy head.

Unique height

A Giraffe's incredibly long legs and necks allow them to feed on leaves high in the treetops, where few other animals can reach. They may be taller than any living animal, but giraffes still have seven vertebrae, or bones in their neck. This is exactly the same number as most other mammals, including humans. However, each individual vertebra is very long. Put together, they produce a tall column, which allows giraffes to feed high above the ground.

Giraffes have a very high blood pressure because of their unique height. Since the head is much higher than the heart, giraffe's hearts have to work very hard pushing blood up into the brain. They pump 19 gallons (73 liters) of blood every minute. The heart needs to be huge and powerful to keep up this work throughout an entire lifetime.

The head is so high that gravity keeps trying to pull the blood downwards. Giraffes have a series of special valves in their necks to stop the blood draining away. Without these valves, oxygen would not reach the brain and the giraffe would faint.

◀ Only the tallest trees are beyond the reach of a giraffe's stretch. This one is in the Masai Mara National Park, in Kenya.

A Giraffe is Born

As she gets ready to give birth, a heavily pregnant female giraffe moves away from the main herd, looking for a quiet spot. Inside her, a calf has been growing for about fifteen months. Like most giraffes, she prefers to give birth in one of the calving grounds that have probably been used by hundreds of others in the past. These areas are dotted around the grassland and look identical to the surrounding countryside. But for some reason, giraffes always return to the same place. Many females remain faithful to one spot each time they give birth.

▼ This baby giraffe has just been born. The mother is licking her calf clean.

GIVING BIRTH

On average, female giraffes give birth to one calf every 20 months. Twins are extremely rare.

•

A female may produce up to twelve calves during her lifetime, but eight is the average.

▼ A newborn giraffe calf is extremely weak and cannot even stand at first.

The birth itself takes between one and two hours. The female does not make matters easy for the calf because she gives birth standing up. The calf's arrival into the world is followed by a 7 foot (2 m) drop on to the hard ground. But since its bones are still soft, the young calf is not hurt by the fall.

The female immediately starts licking the youngster. As well as cleaning the fur, this close contact helps the mother memorize the scent of her calf. From that moment on she will recognize her calf by its smell, even amongst a herd of other young giraffes.

First steps

Newborn giraffes can stand after just 20 minutes. By instinct, the calf nuzzles its mother's teats and begins to suckle. At first its legs are wobbly and often collapse under its body weight. The first few hours are the most vulnerable stage of the calf's life because it cannot run away from predators.

GIRAFFE CALVES

A newborn calf may be 6.2 feet (1.9 m) tall and weigh 225 pounds (102 kilograms).

•

Young males can grow up to 3 inches (8 cm) a month and will double their size within the first two years.

◀ Suckling is easy while the calf is young. But as it grows, the young giraffe becomes too tall to reach its mother teats.

Newborn calves are at risk of lions, cheetahs, hyenas, hunting dogs, leopards, and crocodiles, but the calf quickly learns to walk and can run within a few hours. Female giraffes are very protective and will defend calves against any approaching predator. They attack enemies with powerful kicks that can kill a fully grown lion. But even with this careful protection, 50 percent of giraffe calves die in the first six months of life.

▲ Calves are at most risk from predators that hunt in packs, like these hunting dogs. While the mother drives off one dog, another can creep up behind and take the unprotected calf.

Safety in numbers

The mother and her calf remain alone for about ten days, allowing the calf to grow stronger and improve its running skills before returning to the rest of the herd. At first the young calf tries to stay close to its mother, but when she wanders off to look for food, it joins a group of other young giraffes for protection.

▲ Three young giraffes stick close together in the Masai Mara National Park, in Kenya.

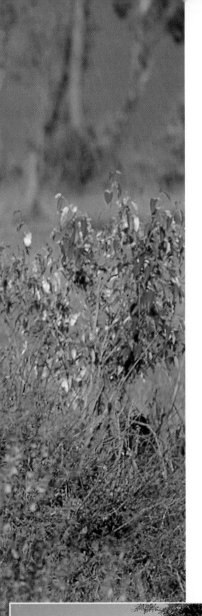

Early warning system

The calf may only be two weeks old, but already it is one of the tallest animals on the African plains. A group of calves together can watch every part of the landscape. They will notice a predator creeping in for an ambush quicker than a single calf. This extra few minutes of warning gives the calves a chance to escape. Young calves alone are much easier prey for predators to catch and kill.

When its mother returns from feeding, the calf eagerly darts beneath her to take a long drink of milk. Calves try eating leaves for the first time when they are around 4 months old. However, they will also drink their mother's milk until they are about 15 months old.

◄ While the calf feeds on leaves from a low tree, its mother scans the surrounding landscape for signs of danger.

15

Learning to Survive

The calf spends much of its first few months playing, running around its mother and chasing other calves. This exercise helps develop the calf's muscles and senses, and lets it learn about the other giraffes who will share its life in the future.

As the calf explores its surroundings, it also learns about the animals that live alongside the herd. Small grazing animals such as gazelles, stay close to giraffes to take advantage of their early warning system. The giraffe's high viewpoint and sharp eyesight help it spot predators at once, and their sudden nervous behavior will alert all nearby animals to the approaching danger.

▼ Like these impalas below, giraffes prefer to drink close to other animals. There are lots of ears and noses to pick up the movement and scent of approaching predators.

Friends and enemies

Flies are a never-ending irritation to the young calf. They constantly hover around its face, taking moisture from its mouth and the corners of its eyes. Tsetse flies pierce the calf's thick skin, using sharp parts in their mouths to drink its blood.

Luckily the calf has the help of small birds called ox-peckers, which hop about on its back and neck eating the flies and ticks. But ox-peckers can also cause problems. If the calf has a slight graze on its skin, the birds are likely to peck at the wound to drink the blood, making the wound worse.

▲ A large flock of ox-peckers like this, can make painful wounds in the giraffe's skin.

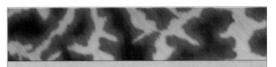

SCRATCHING

Biting insects such as flies, make the calf itchy, but its body shape makes it difficult to scratch itself. Instead, the calf learns to rub itself against trees to ease the itching.

Running away

The calf must always keep a sharp eye out for predators. At the first sign of danger it will try and hide behind its mother. But if she is far away when a predator appears, the calf can run surprisingly fast. Calves have much shorter legs than adult giraffes, but they can move more quickly. Fully grown giraffes are too heavy to sprint from a standing start, while the lighter calves find it easier to dash off quickly when they feel threatened.

◀ A very young giraffe is safest hiding between its mother's legs.

When running, or galloping, giraffes swing their back legs forward first, followed by their front legs. Their legs work differently when walking. Unlike most four-legged animals, which move one front leg together with the opposite back leg at the same time, giraffes walk by moving both legs on one side, and then both legs on the other side. This produces a swaying movement, but it helps giraffes keep their balance and stops them falling over.

Giraffes are one of the few mammals that cannot swim at all. Their unique body design makes it impossible. They have relatively small feet supporting an enormous weight, so they cannot even walk across mud without sinking. For this reason, giraffes very rarely try to cross rivers.

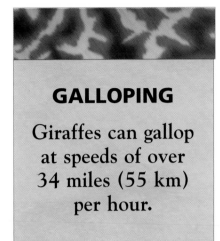

GALLOPING

Giraffes can gallop at speeds of over 34 miles (55 km) per hour.

▼ When a large herd of giraffes starts to run, the ground vibrates as they thunder past.

19

Dangerous sleep

People once believed that giraffes never sleep, because giraffes usually sleep standing up. This made them appear to be awake. Giraffes can sleep lying down but they rarely do, since getting up is a slow business and makes them vulnerable to attack by lions. So they usually sleep standing up for short periods. Giraffes need little sleep and seem to exist on just four hours a night.

When tired and surrounded by the protection of other giraffes, the calf will sometimes lie down with its legs tucked underneath. It sleeps with its head curled round, resting on the flat part of its back, close to the tail. But it only stays like this for just a few minutes before waking up.

When they are about four years old, male calves leave their mother and join a group of other males, who they will stay with until fully grown. Young female giraffes do not leave their mothers. Even as adults, they never stray far from her territory.

▼ Female giraffes often keep calves in open areas, making it difficult for predators to approach without being seen.

GIRAFFE NOISES

Giraffes were once thought to be completely silent. But they do sometimes use their voice. Calves have a sheep-like bleat when they are lost or frightened. Bulls can produce harsh coughs and grunts when preparing to mate.

Finding Food

Giraffes are too tall to eat plants from the ground, so they have to eat leaves growing at the level of their head or above. This is known as browsing. Adult giraffes eat fresh leaves growing in the tops of trees. The young giraffe has no difficulties finding food since there are trees dotted all around the plains. But until they are fully grown, young giraffes are often forced to separate from the adults because they cannot reach the tall trees where the adults feed. They must find lower branches, usually on smaller trees.

▲ Calves take food from much lower trees than the adults. This sometimes takes them away from the main herd and makes them easier to attack.

Male and female giraffes have very different ways of feeding. Bulls, male giraffes, stretch their necks as high as possible and push their heads upwards to reach the highest leaves. Cows prefer to put their heads above the branches and eat leaves beneath their chin. Since bulls are much taller, they take leaves that are too high for the cows. This avoids competition for food, even when a bull and cow are feeding from the same tree.

▶ In the wet season food is plentiful and giraffes don't need to stretch to reach the juicy leaves.

Eating techniques

The young giraffe eats by taking a small branch into its mouth, pulling backwards and combing off the leaves with its teeth. The giraffe's canine teeth are divided, like a comb, which allows it to rake leaves from a branch, instead of picking them off individually. This completely strips the leaves from the stem.

However many African trees, such as the acacia, are protected with long, sharp spines. Leaves from these trees are picked with a lot more caution. The giraffe carefully plucks individual leaves from the branch using its sensitive lips and pushes them back into its mouth.

▼ This giraffe is using its strong tongue to break off a branch and pull leaves into its mouth.

Sometimes the giraffe uses its incredible tongue like an elephant's trunk to grab and pull food. The tongue grows up to 18 inches (46 cm) long and can completely wrap around a small bunch of leaves and rip them from the branch. This technique also collects some of the thorns, but the giraffe never seems to notice. Giraffes can chew and swallow spines that would damage most other animals. The tops of their mouths are grooved and hard to prevent damage and they produce a thick saliva which coats the spines and other food to reduce the chance of injury.

▲ Giraffe country is unmistakable, because the tops of all the trees are flat where the leaves have been eaten.

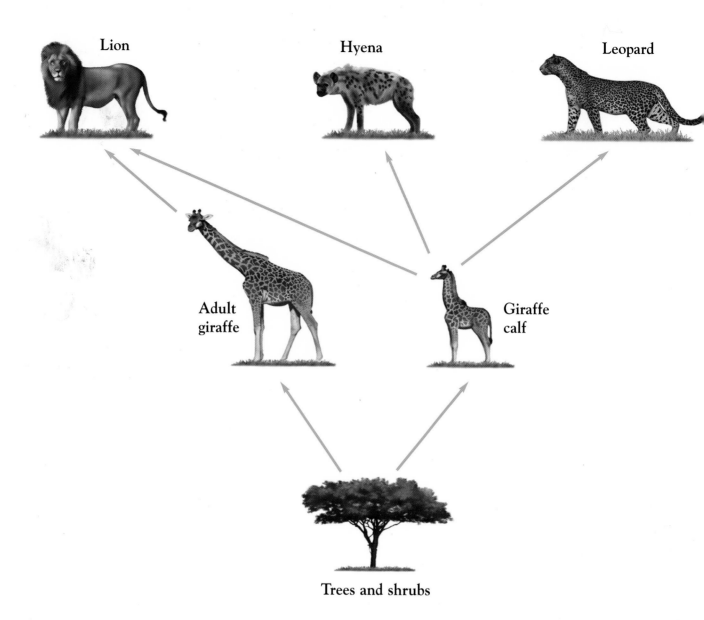

Lion

Hyena

Leopard

Adult
giraffe

Giraffe
calf

Trees and shrubs

Diet

Although leaves form 95 percent of the giraffe's diet, it will also eat fruit, flowers, seedpods and climbing plants, which grow among the high leaves. A giraffe's great height guarantees that it has little competition for food. Monkeys are the only other large mammals that eat in the treetops.

▲ The giraffe food chain is very simple because they eat just one type of food. Calves are hunted by hyenas and leopards, but as they grow bigger, only the lion is a predator.

► Giraffes have little competition feeding in the treetops.

Giraffes need to eat lots of food. Leaves are low in nutrition, so giraffes have to eat large amounts of them to get the energy they need. Male giraffes eat up to 145 pounds (66 kg) of food a day, while females eat up to 128 pounds (58 kg) a day.

Giraffes spend nearly twelve hours a day eating. They feed mainly in the early morning and late afternoon, when the temperature is at its coolest. They will even eat at night, when the moon is bright enough to allow them to see. Between the hours of 10 am and 3 pm, they rest in the shade of large trees, hidden from the heat of the sun. They spend this time chewing the cud, swallowing for a second time the leaves they first ate during the morning.

CHEWING THE CUD

Like cows, giraffes are ruminants, which means they have a stomach with four chambers and an unusual way of digesting food. When a giraffe first chews leaves, they pass into a special stomach chamber. Later, the food is pushed back into the giraffe's mouth and chewed a second time. Only then will it be swallowed and passed into the next stomach chamber, ready for the next stage of digestion. This is called 'chewing the cud'. Giraffes need to chew their food twice because leaves are tough and hard to digest.

▲ Giraffes and elephants share the food near this river in Kenya.

SALT

Giraffes need to add salt and other minerals to their diet. These are collected by chewing special rocks at places known as *salt-licks*. Calves find salt-licks by following the adults.

Favorite food

Giraffes prefer eating fresh leaves, so their movements are controlled a little by the seasons. Trees produce new leaves during the wet season, so during these months giraffes can wander freely around the plains finding their favorite food anywhere. But in the dry season, trees that are out in the open do not send out new growth. During these months, giraffes often move closer to rivers. Near rivers, trees grow new leaves all year round, usually because the tree's roots find water.

Water

Although giraffes have been known to survive for a month without water, they usually drink once every two or three days. Drinking is an awkward process for an animal whose mouth is so high above the surface of a river. To reach the water, the giraffe has to spread its front legs as wide as possible before lowering its neck. This is a very dangerous position, because the giraffe cannot see what is happening nearby or move quickly if there is danger. Drinking is the time when most giraffes are attacked by lions.

▼ A giraffe's legs are longer than its neck, so it cannot reach water without lowering its entire body.

Adult Life

Giraffes are sociable animals that live in groups. However, they do not live in a single, unchanging herd, like many species. They wander the plains in small groups, joining with others for a few days, before separating and moving on. The number and members of each group change almost every day. Each giraffe has its own territory, or range, where it spends its entire life.

By the time he is eight years old, a young male giraffe is about half-grown. He still lives with a group of other males that have no territory of their own yet. At this age, the males begin to test each other to work out which are the dominant animals.

GIRAFFE HERDS

A typical group is made up of between two and six giraffes, but on rare occasions there may be as many as fifty. At the center of each group is an adult female and her calf. She may be joined by lone females of any age, or other adult females with young. Bulls will join the group for a day or more and then leave.

▶ Necking giraffes are simply testing each other's strength, not trying to hurt their opponent.

◀ A single group of twelve giraffes is quite unusual. They will sometimes gather close together when predators are nearby.

Young male giraffes compete in mock-fights almost every day. The fights are slow and non-violent. Each giraffe pushes his opponent to judge his strength. The two giraffes then twine their necks together in a ritual known as *necking*. This allows them to work out which of the animal's are stronger or weaker.

Fighting and displaying

By the time the males, or bulls, are fully grown, they each know their place in the social scale of males. The biggest, strongest male is the dominant bull. He keeps this position with a pattern of behavior called displaying, each time he meets another male. A bull displays by stretching up to full height and pacing around slowly with a strange stiff-legged walk. He stares hard at his rival until he looks away. Then the dispute is over. A dominant bull will probably reach his position without ever once having a true fight.

True fights are very rare and normally only happen when a completely unknown bull appears in a group. As a stranger, he has no established position amongt the males, so the others do not know how to respond to him. Fights might break out, but only to judge the newcomer's strength. The battles are usually over quickly and peace is restored.

▼ Unlike most other animals, giraffes fight in total silence. Many other species produce loud roars and grunts to try to frighten their enemies.

▲ The giraffe has a massive head. It is a powerful and damaging weapon when rammed into the neck of an opponent.

Bulls fight by pushing each other and charging with their heads down. They both try and ram their opponent with lowered horns. Occasionally they hit out with the sides of their heads, but this is unusual and serious injuries are scarce.

Fully grown

By the time he is ten years old, the bull is fully grown and leaves the group to establish his own territory. He needs to find a large area that contains plenty of food, access to water and, most importantly, other giraffes. At first he wanders around, joining groups of other adults for a few days before moving on. Eventually he settles down in one place, where he will stay for life.

The bull should have no problem finding a suitable area for his territory, because male giraffes do not defend their territory or drive off their opponents.

TERRITORY

Adult female giraffes have a territory of up to 404 square miles (650 sq km). Dominant bulls have a much smaller territory, about 47 square miles (75 sq km). Before they find their territory, young bulls wander over a far bigger area than the adult bulls.

▼ Giraffes need to remember every part of their territory. They must know where to find the best food and exactly the right direction to travel towards waterholes.

Finding a mate

There is no set breeding season for giraffes, which means they mate and give birth at any time of the year. Every bull spends a great deal of time patrolling his territory, using his sense of smell to inspect each female to see if she is ready for mating. Females usually mate once every 20 months, but if her calf dies shortly after birth, she will mate again sooner than that.

▲ Male giraffes know when females are ready to breed by the scent of their urine.

When a dominant bull arrives in a group, all the other males leave. He alone will mate. At first, the female avoids him, but he follows her and eventually, she allows him to mate. The bull stays with the female for a few days, mating with her several times. Then he moves on to look for other females.

◄ A male giraffe will follow a female for several days before mating. He stays very close and will not allow other males to approach.

Female giraffes do not fight among themselves. They do have a dominance order, but it only shows itself when they are feeding close together. The highest-ranking cows always have first choice of the best food.

Threats

Lions are the adult giraffe's only wild predator. Working together, a pride of lions can bring down an adult giraffe, but it is a dangerous business. Giraffes can defend themselves by kicking out with their powerful legs, or hitting their enemy with a heavy hoof that is as big as a dinner plate. A single kick from a giraffe can kill most attackers.

▼ A young giraffe will provide enough meat to feed a pride of lions for two days.

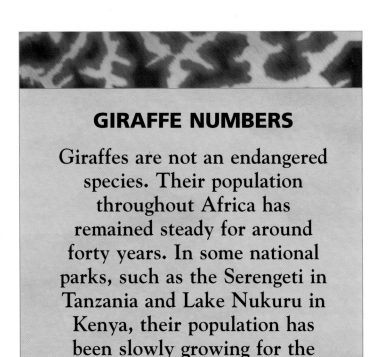

GIRAFFE NUMBERS

Giraffes are not an endangered species. Their population throughout Africa has remained steady for around forty years. In some national parks, such as the Serengeti in Tanzania and Lake Nukuru in Kenya, their population has been slowly growing for the past twenty years.

Giraffes also use their head as a weapon. As they get older, their skull bones become thicker and heavier. An angry giraffe can swing its head sideways at an attacker. Coming down from a height of nearly 20 feet (6 m) a violently lunging head can break a leopard's back.

▲ A gemsbok threatens a giraffe by pawing the ground. The gemsbok is frightened simply by the size of the approaching giraffe.

People and giraffes

Like most wild animals, humans are the giraffe's most dangerous enemy. Ancient drawings from Egypt show that giraffes once lived in North Africa, but their numbers have been drastically reduced by hunting and by turning their habitat into farmland. Today, most giraffes live in national parks or game reserves.

▼ One of these giraffes has been caught in a snare set by poachers. About 5,000 years ago, giraffes were found over much of Africa. Over-hunting has greatly reduced their range.

▲ These bushmen, from the Kalahari Desert in Namibia, are drying out the skin of a giraffe they have killed. Although giraffes are still hunted today, the numbers killed are not enough to threaten the survival of the species.

Meat, skin and hair

Giraffes are still hunted and killed for meat. They are also raised for meat on a few ranches. Tribespeople in Chad and the Sudan hunt them on horseback. Although it can be a long, hard job, a single giraffe will supply enough meat to feed a small village for several weeks. Giraffe meat is legally served in the restaurants of African countries such as the Sudan.

People use giraffes for other reasons. Their thick, tough skin is still used to make hard-wearing sandals. Poachers kill giraffes for the long, black hairs at the end of their tails. These are made into whisks for swatting flies, or hair bracelets for the tourist trade. When poachers kill a giraffe they need to escape quickly, so they take only the tail. The rest of the animal is too large to move and is left for scavengers to eat.

Farmers

Farmers don't usually mind giraffes on their land, because they eat food that farm animals cannot reach. Grazing species such as zebras and gazelles are not as welcome, because they compete with cattle for grass. But as the massive giraffes wander in search of food, they sometimes knock down fences and allow the cattle to escape. Farmers will shoot giraffes when too many fences are destroyed.

Some giraffes learn to feed on agricultural crops such as maize. Once they have discovered this food, they return regularly and farmers have to shoot them to protect their harvest.

▲ This painting, published in a book in 1822, is by an Englishman who visited southern Africa between 1777–1779.

GIRAFFES IN HISTORY

The first live giraffe in Europe arrived in Paris in 1827. As it walked through the streets towards the zoo, the traffic stopped completely. The giraffe soon became the most famous animal in France.

After this first appearance, all the other zoos in Europe wanted their own giraffes. They paid large amounts of money for live animals. By the end of the 19th century, giraffes were found in most major zoos.

▲ Zoos allow people who may not get the chance to travel to Africa to see giraffes for themselves. Until they see them in person, few people can really understand the huge size of a fully grown male giraffe.

Zoos

In the past, many giraffes were captured in the wild and sold to zoos. Most died within a few weeks, but slowly people learned how to feed and care for them in captivity. Today there are giraffes in zoos all around the world. They breed well in zoos and very few are taken from the wild. Giraffes live up to 25 years in the wild. In a zoo they can live up to 28 years.

Giraffe Life Cycle

 **1** Fifteen months after mating, the female giraffe gives birth to a single calf in a safe place away from the rest of the herd.

 **2** The newborn calf stands just 20 minutes later and begins to suckle. It will drink its mother's milk until it is about 15 months old.

3 At about ten days old, the calf and mother join the rest of the herd for the first time. The young calf begins to mix with other calves.

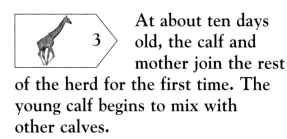

4 At about fifteen months old, the calf stops taking its mother's milk and now feeds from the high treetops. The young giraffe is growing quickly.

5 Females first start to breed when they are around four years old. Males must wait until they are ten. The females live in small groups, but the males are much more solitary.

6 At ten years old, the giraffe is fully grown. It is now the tallest living animal on earth.

Glossary

Browsing (BROUZ-ing) Eating leaves from high trees.

Camouflage (KAM-uh-flahzh) The colour or pattern on an animal that helps it blend in with its surroundings.

Dominant (DOM-uh-nuhnt) The lead animal in a herd.

Dry season (drye See-zuhn) The time of year when no rain falls.

Evolved (i-VOLVD) Developed over millions of years.

Grazing (GRAYZ-ing) Eating plants, mainly grass, which grow on the ground.

Habitat (HAB-uh-tat) The natural home for an animal or plant.

Mane Long hair on the neck of some animals.

Poachers (pohch-urs) People who kill wild animals illegally.

Predator (PRED-uh-tur) An animal that kills and eats other animals.

Prey (pray) An animal that is killed and eaten by other animals.

Ruminants (ROO-muh-nuhnts) Plant-eating animals that have a stomach with four chambers. Ruminants chew food twice before they can digest it.

Saliva (suh-LYE-vuh) A liquid produced inside the mouth to help chewing and swallowing.

Sociable (SOH-shuh-buhl) Animals that live in groups instead of alone.

Suckle (SUHK-uhl) A young animal drinking milk from its mother.

Territory (TER-uh-tor-ee) The area that is defended and controlled by an animal.

Tsetse flies (SET-see flye) Blood-sucking flies that carry sleeping sickness.

Wet season (wet SEE-suhn) The time of year when rain falls heavily and often.

Further Information

Websites

PBS Kids
www.pbs.org
Find out about giraffes and other wild animals.

The Discovery Channel
http://www.discovery.com
Use the search engine to find out information about giraffes.

Encarta Reference
http://www.encarta.msn.com
Find out about giraffes and other great animals.

Books to Read

Giraffes by Jon Bonnett Wexo (The Creative Company, 1999)
Tall Blondes – A Book about Giraffes by Lynn Sherr (Andrews McMeel, 1997)
True Book: Giraffes by Emilie V. Lepthien (Childrens Press, 1997)
Zarafa by Michael Allin (Dell Publishing, 1999)

Index

Page numbers in **bold** refer to photographs or illustrations.